MOTHER/
LAND

MOTHER/
LAND

ANANDA
LIMA

www.blacklawrence.com

Executive Editor: Diane Goettel
Cover Design: Zoe Norvell
Book Design: Amy Freels
Cover Art: "A Mother's Love" by Paula Langstein. Paula is an abstract artist located in
Manhattan Beach, California. Her work can be viewed at www.itspaula.com.

Published 2021 by Black Lawrence Press.
Printed in the United States.

for Noah and Dan

Contents

- already an interesting setup

Inflight Entertainment while the Doomsday
  Seed Bank is Breached   1

I.

Seven American Sentences   7
ARROYO   8
Translation   11
Line   12
ME/AT   15
Sitting by the Hudson   17
Caruru   18
Transa   19
Vigil   20
Madrugada at grandma's   29
Bob Dylan's Prize   31
PB&J   32

II.

Ronald Reagan   37
Fall   39
What I think about when I think about gravitational waves 42
Minute   45
say something   46
Zoológico, circa 1982   47
Vacation Bed   48

Dark room   50
Photograph of water as a mass noun   51
Ode to Wet Concrete   52
Architecture tour   54
Portrait   56
Reno   59
Eclipse   61
FUNJI   62
Every moon   64
spring   65

III.

Mother Tongue   69
Monday between [[impeachment [or something]]
        and the end of the world]   72
Toast to America   74
Portrait   77
Bird   79
Cleaning the Colonial   80
When they come for us on the 7 train   84
Moving Sale   85
Bee   87
BERIMBAU   89

Notes   93
Acknowledgments   96

Inflight Entertainment while the Doomsday Seed Bank is Breached

My son's face is blue
with the soft light of Ice
Age falling on his round cheeks
the voices in the animation contained
by the cups of his child-sized earphones
muffled by the shush of turbines
so constant, so similar to the soothing
sound of waves, we forget the aggression
of their volume

On his screen the body
of a desperate little mammal
is repeatedly crushed by gravity
rocks and metal, the creature still
unable to reach the nut, as its head is smashed
between two stainless steel plates, its eyes bulging
out of their sockets and my son laughs, he understands
what is expected of him now
In this type of movie, there are always good
guys who always win. When we walked in the dim amber
light in the Natural History Museum, surrounded
by bones, we were told we were the sole survivors
the lonely branch of the human family tree
because of our superb adaptability
and we chose to differentiate
ourselves from the dead
with a postfix
"sapiens"

[Handwritten annotations:]
→ blue as metaphor
→ choking, lack of oxygen; sadness
→ line breaks playing w/ meaning + situation — expectations
→ and again
→ word choice + personification
→ line break emphasizing duality of word
"hearing" thus movie describra makes it kind of sad
→ reactions as performative and learned

The picture of the Global Seed Vault
in the Arctic made me think
of architecture and the architect
who said "a vida é um sopro"
life is a breath, at that speed
the floor of the poet's green room
is damp, now wet, now water covers the wrought
iron feet of the bed where she sleeps with her lover

and water fills the Natural History Museum
and we float above the tallest of bone structures
our heads tilt against the ceiling
as we drink from the mouth of a whale
the last sliver of air and I hum
and hold my son's hand
and I think of the cow carcasses
in the drought-cracked soil of the Northeast

The walls in China, Germany, Palestine, the barbed-wired
wall around my mother's condominium and the futile future
walls sprout one after another in an accelerating stop
-motion video, then blur, then crumble
and soon there will be no need for green
camouflage uniforms, gone will be the beautiful
armaments celebrated in the old news, gone is music,
gone is the green of money and the green poetry, gone
were the paintings and recordings in museums, mathematics
gone, long gone have been architecture and those seeds
in the abandoned coal mine in the Arctic

[handwritten annotations:]
Global seed vault → stores duplicates of seed samples from the world's crop collection
climate stuff?
image is delightful for a moment and then tragically sad
more global places and personal macro again. micro — all meet the same fate
this break seems especially deceptive and interesting

On the colorless surface of the moon
imprinted in its sterile dust, undisturbed
by wind or water, there will always remain
a footprint

But for now, I turn my screen to a map of our journey
our airplane tiny, surrounded by blue

so much attention to blue and green
↳ earth colors; also, ice and growth

I.

Seven American Sentences

In the beginning
were people
who lived here
before.

In the beginning
of spring spirits
hovering over the waters.

more fantastical // whimsical premise than above

comma here but not above, why?

The vault
evening, morning, sky
the second
day after a shooting.

the sentences getting less sentence-y

Body: let it serve
as a sign to mark
times, and days and years.

I'm a little lost in the middle here ngl

Correction:
George Washington's teeth
were never made of wood.

In the beginning
of the end
missing
signal for lane change.

undertones of creation, time, exploitation, slavery, predominant // subordinated narratives, but not sure what to make of it tbh

And on the seventh day
same thing again
<u>only some</u>
rested.

a play on the creation myth

ARROYO
— *"Triste Bahia"* —

[handwritten annotations: "→ a steep sided gully formed by the action of fast-flowing water in an arid or semi-arid region"]

[handwritten: "↳ northeastern Brazilian state"]

They say the first
letter of my name evolved
  from a picture of a
                carcass
a cabeça de vaca *[handwritten: a (the?) cow's head]*
  sem as suas costelas *[handwritten: without it its ribs]*
expostas like claws *[handwritten: exposed]*
  or jaws ancient
                    my
neighbor says not to
  let my son sleep
on my bed but I do
            I
  know the terror
        at night we're haunted
by my great great great
                grand-
parents dry on cracked
  soil beating in the cold
of my feet na Bahia in the *[handwritten: at]*
                  bones
  they inhabit on my bed
  In America, I learned
  that arroyos are
              paths
    carved by the rain
    but I already knew
            at

night the cracked soil
   calls for me, as
                cabeças
de vaca of my greats
   calling and calling   *spacing*
                I
   tell them *I don't*
   know you, but I
                do

---

the city's spine
   is a split bifurcation —   *division*
solidified in calcium   *of something as*
                              two branches
                in   *or parts*
   America they
eat the bagasse of
   oranges and say my
                name
means bliss I am
   in love with bone white
concrete, the spine of the
                city
sits fleshless and free

of scales flexible bones
that can bend and bend
                    and
keep bending and keep
bending and bending
bending right up until they
                        snap

After Nathaniel Mackey
and Caetano Veloso

Translation

I wait and weigh the odds
of me being who feeds
and feeds and scrolls through
feeds feeding on grey

→ english or portugese

matter de eu ser um ser que come *of me being a being*
supported by skeleton feeding on *that eats*
feeds que se alimentam de massa *that feeds on grey matter*
cinzenta made of carbon as all living

things sustidas por esqueletos *supported by skeletons*
com suas espinhas vertebrais *with their vertebral spinas*
feitas de carbono como todos os seres *made of carbon like all things*
vivos como a coluna central do lápis *living like the central*
column of a pencil

the ribless spine of pencil
lead pure carbon
os miolos cinzentos dos lápis *the gray brains of pencils*
or graphite and clay

carbono puro eu *pure carbon I*
ser que navega e se alimenta *am the one who navigates and feeds*
de grafite e argila de chance *and feeds on graphite and clay*
de espera de caminho

of chance
on hold   v   *of chance of*
on the way   *waiting, of way*

Line

(handwritten margin note, left): family lineage through passed traits — biological and not pertaining to hands

I inherited from my mother
the knobbly joints and square ends
of my fingers
from my father, I got the habit of biting
my nails
their shortness, the frayed missing skin   *(handwritten): image*
had never bothered me
but now I have a son
and he has begun to bite too

In America, I learned that I can snap
a rubber band against my wrist
each time my hand reaches up
towards the mouth

On the back of my hand
the rubber band disappears
into the color of my skin
but when I turn and face the inner side
it is a clear division
of my body

The first time I saw a cotton tree
I found it beautiful
the cotton so white in its brown cradle
so soft against the square tips of my fingers
I squeezed the dead flower around it
and felt joy
from hearing it crackle

As children, we had cups full of sugar
cane we chewed on it and spit
out the bagasse → *using the same words in multiple*
poems → stylized ||
toothless men ran the knobbly stalks *uncommon languge*
through a machine, the juice
trickled into our glasses
and the flat piece that came out
on the other side
was put through it again
until everything was gone
the dry split stalk thrown into a pile
limp like blond hair

When I first arrived in America, I didn't understand
what people meant when they said
with an American accent that they were
Irish or Italian or French
Now that I understand
I asked my mother for a family *LINE BREAK !!!*
tree
She said
she had never thought of such things
and she wouldn't know much past *how to write about a*
her grandmother's first name *past when it is*
important but not
So what I have is my memory *documented*
of the faces of my relatives
and my own

When I first arrived in America, all I could see
was beauty
the snow fine like sugar *white, blonde, rubber band*
as skin tone and also
white like cotton *division - identifying and*
But now the beauty *simultaneously not*

the land, the tired
metaphors
just make me sad

Before I left for America, I saw an individual
in the mirror
but today, I see my father, my mother, my brothers
my son
and a man missing skin   *oh . . -*
from tears on his back
and the man who did it
When I looked this morning,
I tugged on my rubber band
so hard
that it broke

ME/AT

— "Eu já vivo enjoado" introduction —

In the red light of late
afternoon I stand clean
and naked in the
                post
shower fog with
a bleary reflection
of this body of mine
of yours and I want to
                  call
the conference of my face
summon us from
                this
body of mine of
yours but I don't
              know
how to sift through
the indices of pronouns
in our languages
          I
want you to
confess twisting
the proteins of
            your
mouths masked
in the muscles in
my cheeks as
          I
wipe wet my

[Handwritten annotations:]

me / at v meat
— the poems that have this title format have the //same// structure

↳ i already live sick seasic

who is the you
↳ is the "you" also the self
↳ like a division of the self

→ plural of index

a plural you
The self as a plurality, as a history

hands wrinkled
with condensation
                    and
    stare at this face of
    yours of mine asking
                        what
      have you done
    to us what have we
      done to you can
                    I
    claim you as you
    did one another
                    my
    voice echoes and I get
    closer to the cleared
    path fogging again
    cold silver surface still
                        open
    my mouth and exhale as
                        we
    hide in this meat of me
      this soft present
                    skin

After Nathaniel Mackey
and Mestre Pastinha

Sitting by the Hudson

Rio was never home
until I got far enough
for home to expand into a whole country
Before then
it was just river
in the beginning of a sentence
or in front of a proper name
like Doce

And Rio Doce
was then just water
flowing through a valley
covered with
if not milk
honey
and if not the honey
implied in its name
it was home
if not for me, then
for the men of Mariana
I see crying
on a screen

Mariana Dam disaster
Fundão tailings dam
suffered catastrophic
failure resulting in
flooding that devastated
downstream villages, killing 19
people; the extent of the
damage is the largest ever
recorded with pollutants
spread along 668 km (451 mi)
of watercourses
The failure of the Dam released 43.7 million cubic
meters of mine tailings into The Doce River causing
toxic brown mudflow to pollute the river and
reaches near the mouth when it reached the
atlantic ocean 17 days later. The disaster
created a humanitarian crisis

17

Caruru - brazilian dish

Tea sandwiches sit, pale on their porcelain
plate, their brown crusts cut off
little soggy ghosts and saucer hovering
on the glass coffee table, at home
we would be in the kitchen
the smell faint at first
wading in boiling water with the ochra
but later it would flap with hot dendê, - palm oil
and take flight, glide into the living
room, circle around Tito
and all the primos watching TV
float into the bedrooms
pushing through half open doors
dive down and peck at the noses
of each of the others until they followed
and they would all be crammed together
in the kitchen, among coriander
cashews and shrimp shells a chittering
of voices, insults and laughter, silverware
and the fizz of food being fried.

this one is so sensory

Transa

fuck

My dreams are populated by places
to which I cannot return
parades, people splashing water,
under the sun at high noon
at the edge of rivers de água doce
where the washerwomen carry their loads
on their heads, walking away from the water
towards the shade of short twisted trees
that never shed leaves but gift cocoa or pequi
or cashews, by which I mean the whole fruit
with the juicy flesh that hangs from the nut

But here
I hear my voice
and I sound too much
like myself too much
like Caetano, my tongue wrapped
in plastic, clumsy as it rolls
cold bites of this
language in my mouth
never able to truly taste them
while my son in the backseat
gorges himself

album ?

After Caetano Veloso ("Transa")

Vigil

I.

It took me four years
after having my son
to visit my mother in Brazil
in the new condominium
she had told me
you can actually go
for a walk
outside
at dawn

As we walked
dogs in their electric
fenced yards
took turns accompanying
us, the sky was
peach and pink
and blue
and sliced
by barbed wire
twisted spikes sprouted out of spirals
and pierced the darkening horizon
like the crown set on Christ

The metal tinkled, reflecting
Light from street lamps
from the low beams
of commuter cars
and security

guards in buzzing
motorbikes

Next morning, we walked
the same route, the only route
secured
the dogs came out
in twos
a little one
for alarm or
love or
something else
to be protected
and a big one
for its thick head
of muscle and jaw
birds flew away from their barks
and rested their wings on wire
vines and yellow
flowers intertwined with the fence

II.

Back in America, my friend
tells us, as we watch
the children in the indoor pool,
he left our country
for safety

The children practice
getting out of the water
by grabbing the ground
with their baby hands

bending their fat knees
and dragging their small bodies
over the edge of the pool

My friend whispers
something about kid
nappings, something
about having children now
We nod gravely
and turn back
to the water

III.

Having a child sharpened my vision *line break*
for danger
in corners
in uneven ground
in hot beverages
in dust, pollen and pet hair
in rapidly moving mean *LINE BREAK !*
s of transportation
in water

IV.

Having a child made me lose *AND AGAIN*
Room for animals
They say that pets
resemble their owners
so mine would be a Chihuahua
yelping at any sign of motion

aware of her minute dimensions
of her inability to stop
anyone from crushing her
snappy little bones, just because
they feel like sitting
on her

Kind of funny and also just sad, devastating and strange

and for all her yapping
she would be silent
when lifted above water
pawing the air, her sad little face
quiet, licking
for mercy

V.

At my son's pre-school
they keep a bird
a guinea pig and a rabbit
in rattley cages
in the spring, they brood
eggs under a heat lamp
and learn about the importance
of the right temperature
the strength of shells
the fragility
of the newly hatched

VI.

There were no animals
at his previous pre-school

In the winter, parents and siblings
shed their layers
and settled on their chairs
in the auditorium
Teachers coached the children
on stage
my son played
a drop of water
in a wave
The two of us
the only ones
to retain a tan
like that of the stubborn few
late dry leaves outside
sitting on top of a pile
of snow

VII.

Seasons are reversed
as one crosses the hemispheres
It was warm in the condominium
and in the playground
there was no warning
that surfaces might get hot
Rusty metal squeaked
as I pushed my son on the swings
my mother and I
stretchy smiles on our faces
as we talked in a babying
tone about a new school
where there were
pets

he listened quietly
his shadow moving
back and forth over the tough
grey concrete ground

VIII.

My brother and I were once pulled
by a wave
our limbs pushed the dark water
grabbed at the empty air
I sank into salt
and stayed
still
in the water

I heard
my own throat gasping
and searched for my brother
he was beside me
our mouths open just above
like automated fish
in a carnival game

We made our way to the sand
and stood wet and sniffling
then walked
towards home
crossing the road
to avoid barking strays
our bare feet on the dirt
our long shadows ahead of us

IX.

When we said goodbye to my mother
I gripped my son's hand
and we walked
across the open tarmac
and felt the sun
on the back of necks
as we went up the stairs
that last whiff of hot wind
messing our hair

X.

In the plane, so much talk
about safety
belts, smoking and
slides to be used as rafts
masks
to be slipped over our faces
plastic bags
which may not inflate
we sat far
from the nearest exit
my dress covered in dice *gamble*
and watched through the round edged
plastic window
a body *> line break*
of water against wing
my mother's condominium
smaller
and smaller

then pools
then grids
then crops
then rivers
that looked like veins   *earth as body, as*
mountains   *living ?*
wrinkled like scars

Back in America, I was startled
by the cold
and the loudspeaker
voices that didn't stop
following us
after we got off the plane

XI.

By the pool, two parents talk
about their older children
practicing crawling
processions in their classrooms
and laying under desks
very quiet
very still

XII.

I understood what my friend meant before
though back at home
we would not use the word *safety*
but the word *violence*

XIII.

The trees outside are bare
the landscape devoid
of green
but the sun comes in through the windows
and shimmers of ripples in the pool
we squint and shade
our eyes with our hands

The children line up
and take turns jumping in
then they float
on their backs
like little stars
still in the water
safe

Madrugada at grandma's
early morning

I cut my hair short and I like
that it doesn't fall on your face
making you frown as you scratch
your cheek in your sleep

A dog barks, a motorbike buzzes
and the sounds reach us as if through
liquid, the darkness wet like tar   *images !*
the mosquito zig-zags around you
a halo until it goes silent again, feeding

Your grandmother didn't give us a blanket
and the mosquitos are at it again
So I rip the fitted sheet off the mattress
and as I cover you, you uncurl your limbs
like a flower blossoming with pollen blood

This morning your back was covered
in welts you scratched until you broke skin
ruptures as small as the cut carved
by a tiny buckle on the strap of grandma's
sandal when she hit me once, a wound
I cherished, something visible

You make a sound and I mistake it
for whimpering, but it is laughter
I bury my nose in the fuzz of your curls
my short hair makes me look tired
makes me look like your grandmother

I decide I will grow it out again
I scratch my arm with my teeth
so as not to let go of your hand

Bob Dylan's Prize
— *"You don't know me"* (Caetano Veloso) and *"Fotografia"* (Antonio Jobim) —

you can do us

Eu você nós dois, Caetano
and my boy sleeping in his carseat
já temos um passado, meu
we have a past / die (death ?)
    amor love
His accent and exile songs
like mine expand over
eu você nós you heard us / you can do us
    dois two
the suburban
backyards, quintais, jardins de lá yards, gardens of the
de além, com seus passados and german, with your past
    songs
our song seems to slide off shingles
shake the orange leaves of the trees
eu, Caetano, nós
you   us
        dois two
but our voices are always
confined by a seal of glass
longe do passado que já não temos long past that we don't have
        lá the
fora, a seal of metal e borracha outside ... and drunk /
keep the outside outside the car *e eu* and you   eraser ?
você nós dois, menininho e os nossos you do us, baby boy and
passados divergentes que já our divergent pasts we alredy
        temos have

PB&J

As a foreigner
I was against
it by default

But later
as a mother
I was
to make sandwiches

I turned away
from my American child
to hide a grimace
as the knife
slid on the oily surface
extracting
a hanging grub
the mustard
color of dusty old
mid century velvet couches

I nagged my husband
for separate utensils
fear
of contamination

Then, one day
I was stranded
starving
under a sleeping child

the sandwich still
under his chubby fingers
bitten only once
and about to fall

I moved
my free arm
closed my eyes
as a survivor
on TV
brought it to my lips
and bit

Sweet swirls swimming
in fat
thick, creamy
fat
fromage de meaux
unpasteurized
beautiful body of butter

As I prepared
to bite again
more
than in that citizenship
swearing ceremony
earlier that month
I felt
as an American

II.

Ronald Reagan

Washington
National
Airport
  IATA: DCA | ICAO: KDCA | FAA LID: DCA
02/10/2017
new signs
read Real ID™
at the souvenir shop
new hats, t-shirts and mugs
demand the return
of American
greatness
by the line Clear™
offers a 30-day trial
for fast track crossing
of security in exchange
for money and fingerprints
  my feet are bare
the old x-ray machine
encircles me as I mirror
the outline of a figure
a featureless human
  hands up | hands up | hands up
a woman puts on gloves
and pats down my chest
"buttons", she says
my bag is scanned, swiped
my clothes handled by a man
also in gloves

on the other side
an American LINE BREAK
Airlines™ ad says
they are #goingforgreat
HappyORNot™
asks me to answer
with emoticons "how good
is your wi-fi?"
I stare at the yellow
smiley
I see my name in a list
on a screen
flashing
  stand-by | stand-by | stand-by

Fall

Song

                birds

      rain

down   the

      neighborhood

    not   song

not   feather

    not   rain

but   the   dark

   tarry   weight

of   the   body

    propelled

  to   gravel

by   gravity

Cats   and   dogs

    curious   creatures

they   are

    possible   casualties

residents   keep

    their   leashes

tight on   their   beloved

  pugs,   may   Sally B   rest

      in   peace

An   anchor
   says   it   is   not
just   any
       kind,   no
sparrows,   no
         pigeons
   only   grackles
and   I   say
   there   are   fucking   birds
         falling
   from   the   sky

But   part   of   my   outrage
   part   of   my   wonder
is   faded   by   familiarity
   not   Hitchcock
       not   Poe
but   the   50   o   o   birds   *numbers broken*
   that   fell   before
on   another   season
   another   place
I   had   forgotten
   as   if   its   name
had   not   been
   'New   Roads'
but   'Macondo'
   a   different   disease
a   whole   different   type
   of   epidemic

40

As   I   wait   for people
    in   hazmat   suits
I   am   afraid
    of   forgetting
but   I   am   more   afraid
          of   remembering
The   premise   of   duty
to   bigger   catastrophes
    no longer   works:
    no   gravel
on   that   fall

I   try
    to   think of
        time
    as   an   abstraction
and   stars above the   clouds
    above   the   birds
    as   they   see   us
          as   small
              as   bees

What I think about when I think about gravitational waves

I. Fabric

A pastel pattern of pink
and violet wild flowers
lightly outlined in thin charcoal
on a sheet pegged to the clothesline
rippling in the wind over grass
a girthy woman
stretching out her arms
pinching the four clothespins off
one by one
to set the sheet free
But then she holds two corners
and as if whipping a fly
off the nose of a lion
she rids the fabric of motion
with one
loud
flap

II. Conference

The man in front
of the slide show said
you can see the earth
he said
jiggling like jello

he said
but don't be afraid
he said
and I hadn't been
until he said it
the earth
doesn't really do this
he said
the effect
he said
is greatly
exaggerated
he means
I think
the animation
where said earth jiggles like jello
though the kind of jello one might
find on a Pinterest board
for Earth Day
I googled
all things gravitational
Newton explains
it said
the tides
and I hoped
nobody ever knew
I had never thought
they needed
an explanation

III. Spacetime

All bodies move
to their natural place
The attraction
equal
to the product
of their masses

physics & stuff

divided
by the distance
between them
Listen to their whisper in space
ripples in the fabric of their sheets
waves
as two merge
into one

Minute

What is inside red?
What is inside green?
What is inside me?

What is Earth?
Is Earth in grandma's house?

What is a minute?
Are minutes for cooking?

Is the daytime nighttime
for the moon?

say something

for your safety
if you see something
say
a package
a purse
say something
that should not
be there
unattended
say something
laughing
as they say something
you don't understand
say something
scribbling something
you don't understand
say something
you don't understand
say something
that should not
be something
for your safety
say something
ceasing to be
something
for your safety
if you see something
that should not
be

We were little and we wore white we squinted at all that light we were hungry we were given pink candied popcorn we licked our sugared fingers the air hot and heavy with água doce everything infused in sunlight in a tinge of purple and I don't know if what I recall is that day a blend of different days or a photograph. I remember the sky burned white behind us in a picture but I also see it big and bright blue pierced by spikes on top of the fences that kept us away from the animals but let their sweet musk through to reach us The zoo looked so huge to me then and when I went back with my son I was surprised that it was still huge but now rendered sharp in high contrast the vivid ipê greens and yellows of my Nikon D4s viewed each time as just taken pixels as bright in a future device as on the back of my camera I now show my son chewing with his pink candied mouth I no longer have that old photo of us dressed in white and sometimes I wonder if there was a picture in the first place or if some of it happened only in poetry the purple imposed by a memory that learned to see itself filtered in flare Back home at my parents' we look at the photographs of me as a child now I find her beautiful she looks like my son and I like my mother

Zoológico, circa 1982

Vacation Bed

As not to wake you
I unzipped just enough
to slide my hand
past the hard shell
of the suitcase
As I felt
I forgot
that all I wanted
was a notebook
a pen
and socks
to go for a walk
I made out the outline
of the buttons
on your father's shirt
and the clean soles
of the high heels
I know I'll never wear
then twirled my fingers
around shoelaces
you can't yet tie
and sailed my hands over
the smooth plastic
of a ship
to which I didn't hold the key
I cupped a sleeping lion
stroked its mane
pried open its mouth
and as I felt

its plush little teeth
take a nip at me
you shifted
and I laid the animal
back on its pillow of t-shirts
without a roar
and when you reached
with your little boy hand
towards the space beside you
I was back there already
sucking on the tiny spot
of blood on my index finger
and adjusting the blanket
that kept us
together

Dark room

A small room
vanishes

What is or was
there

the varnished floor
felt by feet

charcoaled shapes
emerge, a lighter gray
bed
surfaces
making
a dark L around it

After George Oppen ("A Theological Definition")

Photograph of water as a mass noun

Learning to expose
a photograph leads to water-
falls, the effect of the shutter
speed easily detectable
slow it down for the camera's
translation of motion into static
liquid to silk to vapor

Dragging the shutter gives
the water about to reach the rock
and the water on top of it
and the water just plunged over
time to come together
into a single frame

Outside the photograph
water keeps coming down,
dark floating on top of more
of itself, white foam, as it splashes
gelatinous and transparent on top of flat rock
slithering down paths carved by its antecedents
roaring as it beats against boulders

and it falls
and it keeps falling when I place
a cap over my lens
walk down the mountain
put a kettle to boil
and drink as I look
at the photographs on my screen
and it keeps falling
as I fall
asleep

Ode to Wet Concrete

grey
magic
levitating
against walls
in rotating drum
or walking on water
in a Palace
of Dawn
Christ
the Redeemer, bed
for Falling Water
bossa
spread flat
by sandal or spatula
sandy grit
scratching blade
mixer of earth and sky
in distant downpour
mixer of sky and skin
on ungloved hands

drying beauty
mask, opaque mirror
holder
of children's
hands
broken
promise
order
uprooted
by roots
the stuff of sculpture
the stuff of sidewalks
the stuff of home
house
where I can fall
asleep
without fear
of burning

Architecture tour

here what you see
is the intent to express
the frame once concealed
with ornament
once unimaginable
here flowers made as if cut
by machine, as cog
rotating hopes here
glass, here metal frame
here limestone, here ground
here unobstructed floor imaginary
walls to let the wind through cave
to its threats
here windows no longer
receded
here modern and post
here you
your weakness for glass
here sky scraped
here water high above
like the tubes in your ears
hear the difference
steel steal still
here words you only know
in English
here curved concrete
you know without language
here bodies burrow under the lecture hall
here's to people with torsos of steel

here's to waiting for clouds
here's to there
the masses
that give them expression
here's to caving
here is to there
winged elbows
eyeholes orange hair
here's to traffic cones
hear britadeiras crashing stone
here brita here bedrock
here now Chicago
here then so many places
here later who knows
here then there now
there the imbalance
in the brooklyn bridge
here the tacky
signage on his tower
here's to your weakness
there there
the masses caving to threats
here's to those super-people
here's to ruins
hear the still
here
stand

After Sylvia Plath

Portrait

I94 rush
hour in Chicago
still bright but that warmth
in the yellow that rembrandt angled
lighting on the buildings the bounce
back pink, blue, gold stain
-ed glass framed by solid I
beams hinted
at sunset

we flowed ahead in our metal
encasings would be still
in a photograph but outside
of a frame
slow and steady as if pushing
through syrup
or tar

a truck approached on my right
and as it made its sluggish way forward
the blue elantra two lanes removed
disappeared swallowed by the truck's
giant white head I chuckled
at the anachronism, the white
T-rex, the glint of metallic
blue of its victim
anything to get me through
stuck moving
lethargically close to getting

somewhere I thought
about the blue
elantra looking
at me how I was
the one swallowed
I imagined the truck cradled
more of us in its cold
blooded flatbed
released them like aluminum
baby reptiles on the road hoping
at least one of them
would make it
in the end

but after creeping
back and forth beside me
it passed
on its back two
square sofa-beige
armored tanks

I gave up
on my gps to take
a crooked picture
and another and another
captions starting
and stopping in my head
I thought I had been
so close
but the tanks
looked so far in the photograph
I got back to navigation
the truck didn't

go away
I saw it still
sometimes briefly sometimes
for long stretches all the way
home it wasn't
a good photograph
the buildings too bright behind the tanks
a pole
the cars distracting
the scale
all wrong
besides everyone
already knew

Reno

Gravel crackles under my shoes
then the quiet sidewalk too
wide for just one, other
humans, prairie dogs in tinted air
conditioned
glass holes

if I fogged up my glasses with my breath
and looked down, it might look like I am
walking on sand
but I don't

the light pleads with me
"wait," "wait," "wait"
then lets me go

on the photograph
on my screen the sky weighs
down on the buildings
and keeps them
short, flat, so different
from New York City
where the buildings won

Trees are engineered
into intervals, grass
patches free
of weeds, concrete sometimes
cracks
but the plants here forget
to rebel, and each crack remains
just a crack

Eclipse

Under the arc of celestial
bodies in their trivial dance
eyes naked, I yawned
and kept moving, unmoved
by their movement, then I looked
down at a crack on the sidewalk
and saw the sun
-dappled light bent
into the shape of the moon
by the moon
asserting herself
in the sky
on the ground
I imagined the moon
could see me, imagined I was
the moon seeing me
small, looking down
at her, trying in vain
to eclipse her, I
so small in the sidewalk
surrounded
by a thousand 'C's

After Ben Lerner (Leaving the Atocha Station)

FUNJI
— *"Sodade"* —

Restaurante Tambarina, Lisbon, July 14, 2018

Oh skin soft wet
  rubber container
pele pelo pêlo para para *skin? ful?*

                    pira *pire*

inside, something
  like funji, I
like because it's skin
                      less
unlike mochi unlike
  pão-de-queijo but
very much like them
                    except
for skin
  prosthetic stickiness
in one, and the
                  other
always cracking
  into crumbs
then dry
          powder
but here me
  inside my skin
so far we
        meet

our bodies
 with their traces
 of the funji and
                  pão-
de-queijo that
 rolled there
there in our mother's
                  tongues

Every moon

has so much to say
as she tucks the charcoal
world under her soft silver
light hushes it rocks
the tide saves it
for when
it wakes
o sul o sol o sal
the translation of a whistle
para ti parara tibum *for you it stopped*
hips hopping hoovering
who is the question
onde anda Andrade *where is*
adrógino antropo *arogynous antnropo*
in an antrum
ou na clarice *or in*
tossing sweating in self
consumption
is the question
to   or
not to   or
is it how
often does
your body
bleed

After Sandra Lim and Oswald de Andrade

spring

it used to be that if i saw something
like puddles of melted snow
the blossoming
pink flowers in the suburbs
and the birds
returning from the open
sky so casually shrugging at the miracle
of cryosleep, i understood spring
as a gift from America
the joy of having something
taken
and returned

it used to be that if i said something
that lead
to laughter released like
children freed from a cage
                          and all that
coy cocktail talk
made me feel
like i was
happy

but now all that chatter, that crowd
in the sprouting outdoor
seating the city's gentri-
fied dry

mud over cement
surfaces
remind me of
       the present
              of naive futures
of past springs

III.

Mother Tongue
11/09/2016

To deal with American
dates my strategy was to tell
myself to do the opposite
of what I thought I should do
This used to work, but now
I no longer remember
what I first felt so strongly
about so I am caught
not knowing for certain
the day I was born
switching my birthday
from June to August
one of two months
when the temperature is right
the other one being July
when I was once certain
my mother was born
but now I am more sure
of its other date though
I still don't know
if the proper way to say it
is "July 4th"
or "the 4th of July"

My son was born in September
2011 and when the well
visit nurses quiz me
confirming

our identity
by declaration
of his birth
date, I always have
to stop myself
from saying
"nine eleven"

My son does not in any other
way remind me of 9/11
that day sad but seen from afar
on a screen didn't belong
to us then, the two of us, then one:
not in America, not a person
yet, neither
for those who count
as a person
a person not born
here, nor for those
who count as person
something not
born but now we
can't escape
its imprint
the proximity
of those digits
even if out of order
or in the correct order
I can't tell anymore

My son doesn't know yet
how dates work
he barely understands the days

of the week, I try
to make him say them
in Portuguese like I do
with all the words
I can still remember
hoping for gains
by attrition, but today
because I didn't know
what to say, but still
wanted him to understand
me because I
was afraid for him
speaking anything other
than the unofficial
official language
of this land
which is not my land
despite the claims
it makes in song
I gave in
and spoke to him
in my broken
version of his
language

Monday between [[impeachment [or something]] and the end of the world]

I have crossed
without looking
many times nothing
hit me this morning
I hummed along
with the engine
in the train caught
myself before I
got too loud
now: later
riding in reverse
the sun still
shines through
dirt on the windows
still springs back
from the glass
like mirror or
blade in my head
I love mixed
metaphors
I brew blade glass
metal and water
in my head
I can't
hear myself in accent
I can't
tell the difference
morning | mourning

luto | luto
I turn
my concoction
into fragrance
perfume | perfume
both
same
speed each
up its own
little nostril
they smell
like clean knife
they smell
like nothing
like dead
sunshine
through glass

Toast to America

Time's hard
I go back
to the toaster
oven
my bread's still   too white
I come back still   too I
don't want it like that
soggy, white, come   back
It's burnt

Open the door
only for
a second or
whatever
just
enough
for me   to
get out
    and in
and stay
here a place
I fooled myself
into calling
home a place
here for only
a second   I
                open&
                gentle&
                polite&
                harmless.

and like
a big bang
    a   billion
            mosquitos
        come   in   and
bite me

Like that
I overstayed
here it went by
so quickly
over
stayed vis-a-vis
a person
in the mirror her
face soggy and toast
hard   to tell
the difference
really from the day
before I
here for
so long
so polite
the whole
time
some see
the face
of Jesus
on their
bread

Time's hard, I had
a baby and everything
here and he walks and

talks
American
come back he's grown
    and gone   someplace
here   or   who knows where
    we'll all be   by then
times   pass
    ports   flint   sparks
        over
        -stayed
        a fool
went by
    so quickly

        burnt.

Portrait

these days
knowing
I am running
late doesn't help
I stand the minutes
switching behind my back
re-read a message
something I sent something sent to me
the speckled darkness
of the kitchen top
the ticking
toaster oven
going going my eyes
feel heavy my legs
I can only move
to pick up a knife

scrape the burnt edges
grab the packed lunch
the keys, the extra sweater
make it
out the door
push the elevator button
again, again, again
a rush justifying
the frozen person before
by the counter

these days if I don't drink enough
water I feel the veins of my legs
at night and it's as if this awareness
hurt though not quite the pain I am used to
a phantom a phosphene
like my own voice
in my head listing
what to do
tomorrow
I can't tell
if it's really there

Bird
Turtle Back Zoo, September 2014

I didn't know what to say
each time we passed by the bird
still sitting on a log on the ground
its white head the only
thing that wasn't dirt brown
when it moved, an almost
imperceptible jerk to the side
startled me having
only seen it static
a plastic statue on Americana
themed cabins in the woods
or inside a seal
trapped on paper in my passport
Do I tell my four year old son
it has no room to fly
that the net over the sky
could never be high enough
Should I cancel our membership
or let it expire as we saw the cage
with a black plastic butter knife
borrowed from the cafeteria
as we walk around
 its cage, silent
a father reaches for his
wallet and shows his son
 the same
  bird
on a   dollar
     bill

Cleaning the Colonial

You were once
so foreign
to me the rattling
and whistling of the radiator
the nooks and cracks collecting dust
your wooden body, so lacking
in concrete, so prone to burning
your exterior covered with scales
Now I kneel
and place
a damp cloth on your skirting
I push into your grooves with my fingers
following them until the end
of the wall
when the cloth is covered
with the lines drawn
by your moldings

I wonder if you have forgiven me
for coming here
and ignoring the contrast
of your trims
despite the protest
of painting professionals
and the prescription
of more experienced parents
I headed
to Home Depot
and made all your surfaces
apartment-white

but I hope you see
the beauty
of this light you let in
through your windows
when you amplify
its reflection
from within

I have also neglected the understanding
that you are meant to be filled
with figurines and tassel
curtains
an inherited empire
settee,
with its claws clinging to hand
woven rugs
that your crooked golden chandelier
is supposed to hover above
a solid
dining table

I have kept you mostly bare
I assure you this spareness is not
for your deprivation
or to expose your many
imperfections
Part of it is that I find you
too beautiful to be hidden
part of it is an attempt
to replicate in you
the unadorned spaces
from the faraway place
that formed me

You see, once I realized
sometime ago that
the crown
emphasizing your front door
was purely decorative
that in spite
of having seen so many façades
similar to yours on tv
I didn't know you
and my love for you then
became more
complicated

Now I complain as I try to grapple
with the muck stuck within
the grid
of the radiator
or within the depths
of the oven
you note that most of my work
is on my own mess
and remind me of my progeny's
crayon, and the scratches
caused by my cheap self-assembly
furniture
I retort that the damage
that predates me
is deeper, more disagreeable
more difficult to address
and I continue to clean
and you continue to uphold
your unmovable frame

But notwithstanding
our differences
I lovingly sweep your strange
wooden floors in the kitchen
I occupy your hollow rooms
and populate them with private song
I realize that now, or soon
no one alive will know you
better than I do

By now we understand
you don't really belong
to me
and I don't really belong
but we have come to accept
that our histories have commingled
and as I do my best
to scrub your stains
I imagine my son
grown, inhabiting
another place
feeling cold
for your concrete
counterparts
always wishing
for you

When they come for us on the 7 train

Past the underground tracks, the railroad rises
our eyes adjust to the sun over Jackson Heights
at the platform, the doors slide open and the winter
comes in with the men in their dark uniforms
silence except for the "please
stand clear of the closing doors," the weight
of their boots sways the car and I raise my hand
towards the pole, but one of the men grabs my
wrist and I feel the cold of his black gloves
against the grooves of my tendons, the cold
crosses my skin, the cold mixes with my blood,
the cold travels in my veins, to my fingertips
to my elbow and my other hand lets go
of my son before the cold reaches him too
I say "I'm an American citizen"
the soft tissue in my mouth cracks with frost
I say it louder
"I'm an American citizen" and the frozen edges
of the words scratch as they move through my throat
I shout "I'm an American citizen" and reflected
on the man's visor, I see my face
I think of my son if they take me
I think of my son if they don't
as he watches me whisper
"I'm an American citizen"
while the others are taken
by the men of ice.

Moving Sale

my husband was afraid of the crash
which pushed so many underwater
I was afraid we were too
in love too heavy with honey to extend
a hand
or flee

ao fugir
meu marido tinha medo da queda
e muito acima dos rodapés nossas mãos
se apoiando, empurrando tantos outros debaixo d'água
um amor pesado com mel demais para oferecer
meu medo de que a gente também

at night I think if we might have to be two
out of three, they must be the ones to run
go without giving
a look back I'm not a good martyr but in fall
I'm useless the least likely to help as the water
rises conducting a fake melody with my cold wrinkled hands

então lavo as mãos
paro para olhar para as duas
abertas boiando na superfície da água
canoas falhas fugindo
devagar a corrente de ainda longe da queda
o raio do círculo centrado em mim estendendo

the faint ripple around my body in water spreading
invisible beyond the immediate radius around my hands
meus pés melados stuck to the ground in the crash
free themselves as the honey dissolves too
tentativa tardia de correr
sem precurssão dampened silent underwater

I drip the memory of milk in the water
watch the white beads swirl out extending
fainter towards the walls and around the goods for the flea
market floating dead just beyond the reach of my hands
stuffed bird old button up shirt vintage chair two
soggy boots and a speaker bursting

with water I wash my hands
keep on washing asking if we were to be none instead of two
I should have begged them not to flee stay with me for the crash

Bee

My speech is a dance
its shape approaching
a lemniscate, the buzzing
a mere side effect, for some
my name is homophonous
with copula, a link devoid of me
-aning, but they called me
'Queen' and I carry
my whole hive in my body

They called me 'Queen'
but now in winter, I burrow alone
pregnant with grief underground
and sit still as snow falls
as my veins fill
with anti-freeze
Outside, the cold
cuts, slices and sucks the warm
breath out of bodies then takes
it away in the wind
Outside, all my daughters
are dead

My veins fill and I can
no longer think
of spring, next winter
these babies will die too

survival isn't a gift
isn't a blessing,
survival
is duty

Outside all my daughters
are dead, and I carry
them all in my body

BERIMBAU
— *"Eu ja vivo enjoado" up to "quebra"* —

O sopro é do vento
  we keep moving sopro
  and voice pass and later
    and earlier chords always
                take
  a turn to the percussive
  or if they stay it's in service
  of the beat of running
  the percussion of meat
    and bones cracking
              dirt
    and when we press
  the chamber of the cabaça
  seca against our stomachs
    tighten the wire around its
               neck
    stretch it taut before
  striking with our sticks we
             run
    clandestinos hiding in the
  dark or light or stringing
             wire
    in streets full of tourists
  or accompanying the
             mouths
  of gringo instructors
  who go ginga ginga ginga
  asking Angola or regional
            singing

along with the radio
um pedaço de arame
 um pedaço de pau de pé
               in

 Toque de Angola
 Toque de São Bento
 Pequeno Grande e de
Bimba Toque de Iuna we
                   follow

        o compaço de aço
   o compaço do passo
   o compaço da culpa do
             sol

After Nathaniel Mackey
and Mestre Pastinha

Notes

"Architecture tour" makes reference to the following lines of Sylvia Plath's poem "Brasilia": "Will they occur, / These people with torso of steel / Winged elbows and eyeholes / Awaiting masses / Of cloud to give them expression, / These super-people!"

"ARROYO," "BERIMBAU," "FUNJI," and "ME/AT" are in Nathaniel Mackey's poetic form seen in his collection *Splay Anthem*. As in *Splay Anthem*, the poems are reactions songs (indicated beneath each title).

"Bee" was written after reading about bee hibernation (in which only the queen hibernates, and the rest of the hive freezes to death) in the children's book *Over and Under the* Snow by Kate Messner.

"BERIMBAU" uses lines from the song "Berimbau" by Pierre Onassis e Germano Meneguel of the Afro-Brazilian music group Olodum: "Um pedaço de arame/ um pedaço de pau." It also makes reference to Chico Buarque's song "As Caravanas," which in turn refers to Albert Camus' *The Stranger* in the following lines of the original song "a culpa deve ser do sol."

"Eclipse" adapts the lines "Under the arc of the cello" and "I imagined the passengers/ Could see me, imagined I was/ A passenger that could see me/ looking up..." from an untitled fictitious poem in Ben Lerner's novel *Leaving the Atocha Station* (named after the John Ashbery poem of the same title). The fictitious poem itself in turn adapts the line "Under the arc of the sky" from Lorca's poem "Seville."

"Every moon" begins with a verse from Sandra Lim's poem "A Tab of Iron on the Tongue": "Every moon has so much to say." It also borrows from the title and the ends of the following lines from Oswald de Andrade's poem "Hip! Hip! Hoover!": "América do sul / "América do sol / "América do sal" (South America / Sun America / Salt America) and it refers to the song "Whistle While you Work" in Walt Disney's 1937 film "Snow White the Seven Dwarfs" and the Portuguese translation of the whistle in the song "Heigh Ho" ("parara tibum") in the same movie.

"Fall" was written as a response to news of birds falling dead at a neighborhood in Boston and in New Roads (https://www.theguardian.com/us-news/2016/sep/10/birds-fall-from-sky-in-boston-die-of-unknown-cause and http://www.reuters.com/article/us-louisiana-birds-idUSTRE7034DG20110104).

"Inflight Entertainment while the Doomsday Seed Bank is Breached" is based on news of a breach on the Global Seed Bank in May 2017 (https://www.theguardian.com/environment/2017/may/19/arctic-stronghold-of-worlds-seeds-flooded-after-permafrost-melts and https://www.theverge.com/2017/5/19/15664298/svalbard-global-seed-vault-norway-doomsday-climate-change).

"Mother Tongue" was written as a reaction to the announcement of Donald Trump's victory in the early hours of 11/9/2016.

"Moving Sale" loosely uses a sestina structure, with the expected repeated words containing translations and re-translations instead of plain repetition.

As in John Ashbery's poem/s "37 Haiku," each stanza on "Seven American Sentences" can also be read as an independent 17 syllable poem (in Allen Ginsberg's American Sentence poetic form).

"Sitting by the Hudson" was a response to news of the rupture of a dam releasing toxic mud over Valle do Rio Doce, Brazil (http://www.scientificamerican.com/article/brazil-mine-disaster-floods-area-with-toxic-substances/).

"Transa" borrows the phrase "I hear my voice" from Caetano Veloso's line "I hear my voice among others," in the song "It's a Long Way" from the album "Transa" (1972).

"Translation" loosely uses a pantoum structure, with the expected repeated lines containing translations and re-translations instead of plain repetition.

Acknowledgments

Thank you to everyone in the following publications and presses, where some of the poems in this book first appeared:

The Acentos Review ("Mother Tongue" and "Bee")

The American Poetry Review ("Vigil" and "PB&J")

Birmingham Poetry Review ("Inflight Entertainment while the Doomsday Seed Bank is Breached," "Seven American Sentences," and "Photograph of water a mass noun")

Bull City Press ("Dark room" in the micro-chapbook *Amblyopia*, INCH 45)

Colorado Review ("Eclipse")

The Common ("Translation")

Connotation Press ("Cleaning the Colonial")

Hobart ("Caruru," and "Zoológico circa 1982")

Hayden's Ferry Review ("BERIMBAU," also in *Poets.org* and *Divine Feminist, An Anthology of Poetry and Art by Womxn and Non-Binary Folx*)

The Heavy Feather Review ("say something")

Jubilat ("ARROYO," also in *No Tender Fences: An Anthology of Immigrant & First-Generation American Poetry*)

Juked ("Ode to Wet Concrete")

The Offing ("Fall" and "What I think about when I think about gravitational waves." Also in *LIGO Magazine*)

Origins ("Bird," "Sitting by the Hudson," and "Vacation Bed")

Oxidant | Engine - Box Set Series ("Portrait," "Portrait" and "spring")

Palette Poetry ("ME/AT")

PANK ("Madrugada at grandma's")

Paper Nautilus ("Every moon" in the chapbook *Translation*)

Pigeon Pages ("Monday between [[impeachment [or something]] and the end of the world]")

Rattle ("Line")

Rattle - Poets Respond ("When they come for us on the 7 train," also in *Queensbound*)

Salamander ("Architecture Tour")

Sugar House Review ("Ronald Reagan")

Superstition Review ("Transa")

Written Here: The Community of Writers Poetry Review ("Reno")

Writing this terrifies me. I know I cannot do justice to the people I mention or to my gratitude towards them. I know I will (temporarily) forget someone or many people. The wise choice here would be to go for something minimal and all-encompassing. But I am bursting with love and gratitude to so many people, and I want to try to acknowledge them, however imperfectly.

Thank you to my wonderful editor Diane Goettel and everyone at Black Lawrence Press for selecting this book for the Hudson Prize and all your beautiful work ushering it into the world. I am honored and so lucky.

Thank you to my Maplewood writers' group (a.k.a. WAAK), who heard many of these poems first, for your support, insight, laughter, and love. Without you, this book would not be here.

Thank you to all my friends and teachers at the Rutgers University, Newark MFA Program for nurturing me and my writing. Thank you to my advisor John Keene for the careful and generous reading of my work and the inspiration he provides as a writer, a teacher, and a person. Thank you Cathy Park Hong and Rigoberto González for reading this work and for your words, guidance, patience, and support. Thank you to my cohort and overlapping cohorts. (I love you all). Thank you, Melissa Hartland (aka Heartland) for orienting even the most disoriented among us and for many laughs.

Thank you to the Sewanee Writers' Conference for the great generosity, friendship, and magical times. Thank you to Marylin Nelson and Sidney Wade, for your reading and commenting on some of the work in this manuscript. Thank you so much to all the staff, with a double shot of thanks to the original fellow #swcbar crew.

Thank you to my workshop friends, faculty, and everyone at Disquiet, Tin House, The Community of Writers, and Breadloaf Conferences for feedback on some of these poems, for teaching me so much, and for lasting memories and friendships.

Thank you to the amazing women at the H.S. writing group. Thank you to all the teachers, editors and friends who have helped me with these poems or supported my work, with special thanks to Julia Kolchinsky Dasbach for her thoughtful and kind words for the back cover, for her beautiful work and all she does for me and so many other poets.

Thank you to all the reading series, the self-less people who run them, and their audience, who let me share these poems with them.

Thank you to my loves, my life, Noah Shiber and Dan Shiber, for everything.

Thank you (and I am sorry) to all the people who should also be here, but I failed to mention. And thank you for reading. I am so grateful to you all.

Ananda Lima's collection *Mother/land* is the winner of the Hudson Prize. She is also the author of the chapbooks *Translation* (Paper Nautilus, 2019, winner of the Vella Prize), *Amblyopia* (Bull City Press - INCH, 2020), *Tropicália* (Newfound, 2021, winner of the Newfound Prose Prize), and Vigil (*Get Fresh Books*, 2021). Her work has appeared in *The American Poetry Review, Poets.org, Kenyon Review Online, Gulf Coast, The Common,* and elsewhere. She has an MA in Linguistics from UCLA and an MFA in Creative Writing in Fiction from Rutgers University, Newark.